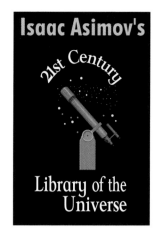

Isaac Asimov's
21st Century
Library of the
Universe

Fact and Fantasy

What Killed the Dinosaurs?

BY ISAAC ASIMOV
WITH REVISIONS AND UPDATING BY RICHARD HANTULA

Gareth Stevens Publishing
A WORLD ALMANAC EDUCATION GROUP COMPANY

Please visit our web site at: **www.garethstevens.com**
For a free color catalog describing Gareth Stevens Publishing's list of high-quality books
and multimedia programs, call 1-800-542-2595 (USA) or 1-800-387-3178 (Canada).
Gareth Stevens Publishing's fax: (414) 332-3567.

Library of Congress Cataloging-in-Publication Data

Asimov, Isaac.
    What killed the dinosaurs? / by Isaac Asimov; with revisions and updating by Richard Hantula.
       p. cm. — (Isaac Asimov's 21st century library of the universe. Fact and fantasy)
    Includes bibliographical references and index.
    ISBN 0-8368-3955-2 (lib. bdg.)
    1. Dinosaurs—Juvenile literature. 2. Dinosaurs—Extinction. I. Hantula, Richard. II. Title.
QE861.5.A85   2004
567.9—dc22   2004048237

This edition first published in 2005 by
Gareth Stevens Publishing
A World Almanac Education Group Company
330 West Olive Street, Suite 100
Milwaukee, WI 53212 USA

Revised and updated edition © 2005 by Gareth Stevens, Inc. Original edition published in 1988
by Gareth Stevens, Inc. under the title *Did Comets Kill the Dinosaurs?*. Second edition published in
1994 by Gareth Stevens, Inc. under the title *Death from Space: What Killed the Dinosaurs?*.
Text © 2005 by Nightfall, Inc. End matter and revisions © 2005 by Gareth Stevens, Inc.

Series editor: Betsy Rasmussen
Cover design and layout adaptation: Melissa Valuch
Picture research: Kathy Keller
Additional picture research: Diane Laska-Swanke
Artwork commissioning: Kathy Keller and Laurie Shock
Production director: Jessica Morris
Production assistant: Nicole Esko

The editors at Gareth Stevens Publishing have selected science author Richard Hantula to bring
this classic series of young people's information books up to date. Richard Hantula has written
and edited books and articles on science and technology for more than two decades. He was
the senior U.S. editor for the *Macmillan Encyclopedia of Science*.

In addition to Hantula's contribution to this most recent edition, the editors would like to
acknowledge the participation of two noted science authors, Greg Walz-Chojnacki and
Francis Reddy, as contributors to earlier editions of this work.

Printed in the United States of America

1 2 3 4 5 6 7 8 9 09 08 07 06 05 04

Contents

• What Killed the Dinosaurs? •

We live in an enormously large place — the Universe. It's only natural that we would want to understand this place, so scientists and engineers have developed instruments and spacecraft that have told us far more about the Universe than we could possibly imagine.

We have seen planets up close, and spacecraft have even landed on some. We have learned about quasars and pulsars, supernovas and colliding galaxies, and black holes and dark matter. We have gathered amazing data about how the Universe may have come into being and how it may end. Nothing could be more astonishing.

Facts about the Universe aren't always about the faraway. Right here on Earth, there were once giant animals called dinosaurs. About 65 million years ago, they vanished. The cause of their disappearance may have come from outer space. Out there we may discover not only the secret of the dinosaurs end, but also learn about dangers that could threaten our Earth in the future. By learning more about space, perhaps we will be able to escape those dangers.

Days of the Dinosaurs

Once, millions of years ago, animals called dinosaurs walked on Earth. Some of them were as small as a chicken. But some were enormous. The largest may have been more than 100 feet (30 meters) long, and the heaviest may have weighed as much as 100 tons or more — about the same as twelve African elephants. The biggest dinosaurs were plant eaters, but the dinosaur pictured here, *Tyrannosaurus,* was a meat eater. *Tyrannosaurus* was one of the most terrifying dinosaurs that ever lived. It was up to 50 feet (15 m) long, and was heavier than most elephants. Its head could be up to 5 feet (1.5 m) long, and its teeth could be as long as 7 inches (18 centimeters).

Opposite: If people had lived in the state of Montana when this *Tyrannosaurus* did, the dinosaur could have swallowed them whole.

Were some dinosaurs warm-blooded?

The dinosaurs were reptiles. All the reptiles that are alive today — such as turtles, lizards, snakes, and alligators — are cold-blooded. This means that when the weather is cold, they are cold, too, and become very sluggish and slow in their movements. But were dinosaurs also cold-blooded?

There are scientists who think that at least some dinosaurs were quite active in the cold and were warm-blooded. After all, birds and mammals are descended from reptiles, and they are warm-blooded. But so far, there is no way to tell for certain if dinosaurs were warm-blooded.

Mighty Rulers of Earth

The dinosaurs first appeared about 230 million years ago. For 150 million years or so, they ruled Earth. Some kinds died out, and others came into being. Then, about 65 million years ago, they all died out, along with many other types of animals and plants. All we have left as evidence that the dinosaurs existed are fossil remains, such as bones, teeth, and footprints.

Why did the dinosaurs disappear? Scientists have come up with various theories, such as that the climate changed, or small animals began eating dinosaur eggs, or a nearby exploding star showered Earth with deadly radiation.

Right: The size and depth of a footprint can reveal how much a dinosaur weighed.

The biggest dinosaur of them all?

It's hard to say exactly how big the largest dinosaurs were. In many cases, sizes have to be estimated on the basis of just a few bones — since that's all that scientists have found. In 1994, some fossil bones from a new kind of dinosaur were discovered in Oklahoma.

Named *Sauroposeidon*, it was not the heaviest dinosaur ever found, but it may have been the largest known land animal of all time. It had an extremely long neck and was believed to stand 60 feet (18 m) tall — about the same as a six-story building.

Above: These dinosaur fossils are in a quarry wall that was once under the ground.

Above: The Barringer Meteor Crater near Winslow, Arizona, is about .75 mile (1.2 kilometers) across. Scientists think it was created by a meteorite impact fifty thousand years ago.

Mysterious Encounter

Scientists have found a layer of rare material called iridium in rocks that are about 65 million years old — that is, the layer was formed at about the time the dinosaurs became extinct. There is more iridium in rocks this age than others.

Iridium is not often found in rocks on Earth. It is more common in materials from outer space. Where did the iridium come from?

Possibly it came from meteoroids, which are rocks that move through space and sometimes collide with Earth. When they enter the atmosphere, meteoroids become fiery "meteors." Some burn up, but some end up on Earth's surface and are called meteorites. The large ones leave a crater, or hole, where they land. Some craters are so old that they have worn away, but scientists can detect signs of these craters when doing research from the air.

Above and right: One of the world's most beautiful craters is Wolfe Creek Crater in Western Australia. It is about 2,800 feet (850 m) wide.

If the Sun's heat and light were blocked by huge amounts of dust in the air, Earth would have become cold and dark. These kinds of conditions would have killed off many plants and animals.

A World Gone Cold and Dark

Could something that struck Earth 65 million years ago have killed the dinosaurs? Many scientists think so.

One possibility is that if the object was big enough, it could have gouged out a huge quantity of rock and soil, ground it into dust, and flung that dust high in the air for miles and miles. The dust would have spread all over Earth. It would have blocked much of the sunlight. Little light or heat would have reached Earth's surface for months or even years. Many plants would have died, and then large animals, such as dinosaurs that ate plants or other animals, would have died.

Smaller animals might have nibbled at bark or seeds or eaten the frozen bodies of larger animals. Some of the smaller animals would have survived. But the large dinosaurs would have all died out.

On a Collision Course?

Are there large objects in space that could possibly hit Earth? Yes. Many scientists think that for an object to cause worldwide damage, its width, or diameter, would probably have to be greater than 0.6 mile (1 km). Scientists estimate there are more than 1,000 objects of this size with a path, or orbit, around the Sun that brings them to within a few million miles of Earth.

Several hundred of these "near" large objects have already been discovered. None of them are expected to come dangerously close to Earth, according to scientists who have calculated the objects' orbits.

But it still is possible that a large object from space might crash into us one day – just as an object may have crashed into Earth 65 million years ago. One reason for this possibility is that the orbits of the known near-Earth large objects might change as a result of the gravitational pull of other planets in the Solar System. Another reason is that scientists have no way to predict the future paths of the many large objects that are thought to exist but have not yet actually been detected.

Some comets and asteroids travel dangerously close to Earth. In this picture, the orbits of a couple of these comets are in yellow, and those of a couple of these asteroids are in red. Earth is indicated with an arrow.

A dinosaur watches a fiery object plunge from the sky. The object, once a meteoroid traveling in space, was lured toward our prehistoric Earth by Earth's gravitational pull (*inset, left*) and became a bright meteor when it entered the atmosphere (*inset, right*). Many scientists think the dinosaurs' disappearance resulted from the collision of a large object with Earth.

Damage from High in the Sky

An object doesn't have to actually strike Earth's surface to do a lot of damage. If a comet or asteroid were to collide with Earth, it would probably hit at enormously high speeds. The pressure of speeding through the air could actually tear the object apart with an enormous explosion.

On June 30, 1908, a forest near the Stony Tunguska River in the middle of Russian Siberia was struck by something that seemed to come from the sky. Every tree was knocked down in an area of some 800 square miles (2000 sq km), and thousands of reindeer were killed. Few people lived in that remote region, and it is not known if anyone died. No crater was ever found. Scientists now believe that the damage was caused by the explosion of a small comet or asteroid high in the atmosphere.

Above: An area near the Stony Tunguska River in Siberia, Russia, photographed many years after the 1908 explosion of a comet or asteroid in the atmosphere.

Comets — a sign of doom?

In older times, people did not really know what comets were. They often thought a comet was a warning from the heavens of an upcoming disaster. After seeing a comet, they thought a war would come, a plague would rage, or a king would die. Of course, even when a comet didn't appear, terrible events like that happened. Somehow, people never seemed to consider that fact.

An artist imagines an asteroid or icy comet vaporizing as it speeds through Earth's atmosphere toward Siberia, Russia.

15

An artist's view of the explosion of a small asteroid that was reported above the Lake Michigan area of the United States. The lights of Chicago, Illinois, can be seen *on the left*.

The View from Space — It's a Blast!

Between 1975 and 1992, spy satellites launched by the United States government observed 136 explosions (about 8 each year) high in the atmosphere throughout the world. The explosions had an energy of at least 1 kiloton — that is, they were about as powerful as a small nuclear bomb. They were created by small asteroids or similar objects that entered the atmosphere. Scientists think such explosions actually occur much more often than reported by the satellites — according to some estimates, there may be as many as 80 a year.

Many of the explosions seen by the satellites were probably only about 50 feet (15 m) or so across. Most of them were much smaller than the Tunguska explosion and weren't even noticed from the ground. But one that occurred over the Pacific Ocean may have flashed as bright as the Sun.

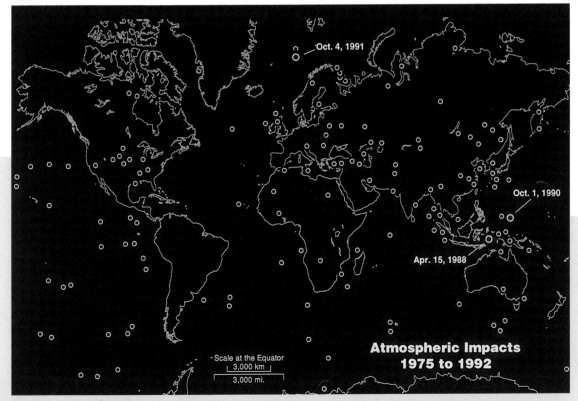

Above: This map shows the locations of 136 explosions caused by small asteroids or similar objects high in the atmosphere between 1975 and 1992. Maybe one occurred above your hometown!

17

The Cosmic Shooting Gallery

We know comets can hit planets because we saw it happen in 1994. In July of that year, a comet named Shoemaker-Levy collided with Jupiter. The comet hit the far side of the planet. As the planet turned into view, astronomers could see the spots where the comet had hit just a few hours before!

Above: This picture of Comet Shoemaker-Levy shows that it is actually in several different pieces, pulled apart by Jupiter's strong gravity.

Above: A close-up view of the heavily cratered surface of Jupiter's moon Callisto. Jupiter's moons have often been hit by objects from space. Perhaps some of the craters on Callisto were made by comets like Shoemaker-Levy.

Comet Shoemaker-Levy striking Jupiter.

Ground Zero — Found!

Could scientists find the crater of an object that hit Earth 65 million years ago? The surface of the planet can change a great deal in all that time, and many old craters have disappeared as mountains have grown and the oceans have changed the craters' shapes.

But geophysicists, scientists who study Earth's features, found signs of an enormous crater beneath the Yucatan Peninsula of Mexico. The crater, called Chicxulub, is invisible to the eye, but scientists detected it with the help of special instruments. It turned out that the crater was created at about the time the dinosaurs disappeared.

Many scientists believe that when a comet or asteroid struck Earth and created Chicxulub, it set off a chain of devastating events that probably wiped out the dinosaurs along with many other types of plants and animals.

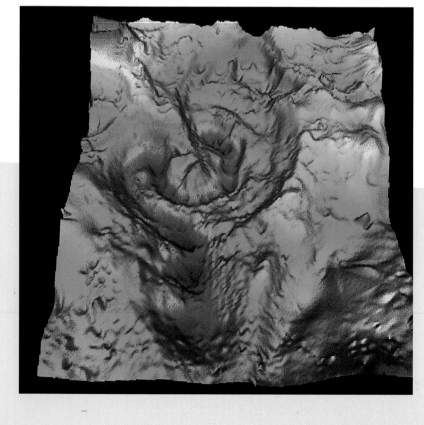

Left: The various colors in this computer-enhanced picture show tiny differences in gravity in the area of the Chicxulub Crater. These differences are arranged in a circular pattern, forming a ring about 110 miles (180 km) across. This "gravity ring" is caused by material piled up by a huge impact at the site 65 million years ago.

Above: When a comet or asteroid hit Earth 65 million years ago and produced Chicxulub Crater, the impact lifted into the atmosphere huge amounts of dust, which blocked out the Sun. The impact probably also caused a colossal wave that reached several hundred miles away.

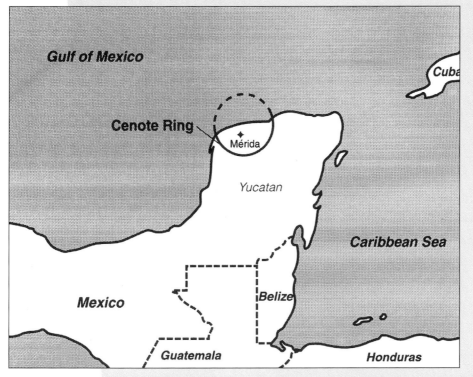

Left: Location of the crater that was created when a comet or asteroid hit Earth 65 million years ago. Many scientists think this impact led to the extinction of the dinosaurs, along with other types of plants and animals. Today, the crater lies buried beneath the surface. Evidence of its location and size is provided on the surface by a ring of sinkholes, or "cenotes."

Kuiper Belt and outer Solar System planetary orbits

Orbit of Binary Kuiper Belt Object 1998 WW31

Pluto's orbit

The Oort Cloud of comets is located very far from the Sun – much farther than the Kuiper Belt (a collection of bodies beyond Neptune, some of which, like the object called 1998 WW31, are actually "binary" objects, that is, they have a moon). Scientists think the Oort Cloud may be the source of some comets that come close to Earth's orbit.

The Oort Cloud (comprising many billions of comets)

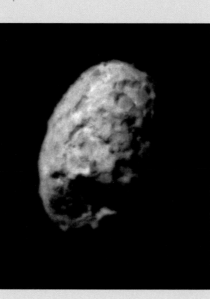

Left: Comet Wild-2, in a side view photographed by the NASA space probe Stardust in 2004. The comet measures about 3 miles (5 km) across.

The Oort Cloud — The Beginning

Although comets, as far as is known, do not get as large as the biggest asteroids, they may travel much faster when they enter our part of the Solar System. If a comet were large enough, it would punch right through the atmosphere and gouge out a crater like the one found in Mexico. Some scientists think it was a comet, rather than an asteroid, that led to the death of the dinosaurs.

A Dutch astronomer, Jan Oort, believed there are billions of comets slowly orbiting the Sun at a distance many times greater than the planets. This "Oort Cloud" might be where some Earth-colliders start their journey.

If a star happens to pass relatively close by, its gravity might pull comets out of the Oort Cloud and send them in the direction of the inner part of the Solar System, where Earth is located.

Above: A Stardust image of Comet Wild-2 that was specially processed to show the streams of gas and dust coming from the comet's surface.

Comets — a look back in time?

Our Solar System formed out of a cloud of dust and gas. We cannot be sure exactly what the cloud was made of. Over billions of years, the Sun and planets have changed a great deal. But scientists think many comets may be made of original matter that has not changed with the years. That is one reason researchers were excited when spacecraft passed near Halley's Comet in 1986. It was the first time a comet was studied up close. Other comets that spacecraft have approached include Comet Borrelly in 2001 and Comet Wild 2 in 2004. Such studies of comets may help us learn more about the beginnings of our own Earth.

Clockwork Disasters?

Some scientists think that every 26 million years or so, like clockwork, comets from the Oort Cloud hit Earth and cause different kinds of life-forms to die out. It isn't hard to imagine a large comet striking Earth. But what could cause collisions to occur, like clockwork, every 26 million years? Certain scientists have developed three theories, but many other scientists doubt that any of the theories are correct. In fact, most scientists do not believe that comets strike Earth in regular showers at all.

One theory – perhaps the Sun has a small companion star. Such a star could pass through or near the Oort Cloud, sending comets toward Earth.

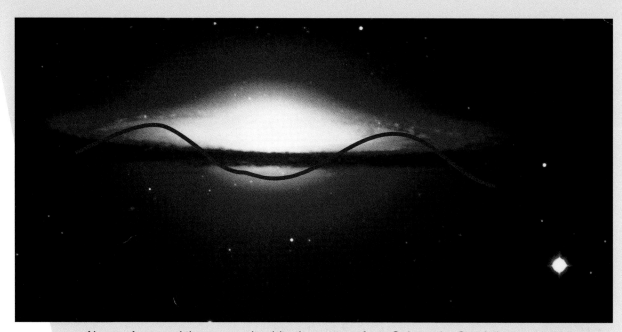

Above: A second theory – as it orbits the center of our Galaxy, the Sun follows a slightly wavy path, first above the middle of the Galaxy, then below it. Every time the Sun passes through the midline, a stronger gravitational pull could send comets toward Earth.

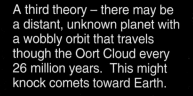

A third theory – there may be a distant, unknown planet with a wobbly orbit that travels though the Oort Cloud every 26 million years. This might knock comets toward Earth.

Diverting Disaster

If the theory of collisions every 26 million years turns out to be correct, Earth is about halfway in time between major comet strikes. Earth might be hit by a body from space at any time, of course. But the real danger may not come for another 13 million years.

Will that be the end of human beings? Maybe not. By that time, we might have colonies on various bodies in the Solar System, and we might have cities built in space.

Wherever we are, we could be watching for the approach of any dangerous body. We might be able to push it aside, or perhaps even destroy it with advanced technology. Then we'd be sure that no collision from outer space could kill *us* the way it killed the dinosaurs.

Above: An idea for a future space colony that could be home to ten thousand people and would be located 250,000 miles (400,000 km) from Earth. It would be constructed out of ore mined from the Moon.

Above: If comets are going to hit Earth in just 13 million years, maybe we should plan to be in space when they arrive! Scientists and engineers have come up with ideas for permanent colonies in space. These colonies could be on other planets, such as Mars, or in outer space itself. This colony looks like a giant wheel (*left*). A large mirror (*right*) directs sunlight into the colony.

Left: If you look carefully, you will see that this proposed space colony has a bridge like the Golden Gate Bridge in San Francisco, California. In this picture, city lights are reflected in the large, mirrored panels that direct sunlight into the colony.

Fact File: What Killed the Dinosaurs?

Why Did the Dinosaurs Die Out?

Possible Causes	Possible Effects
Changes in climate	Some types of plants disappeared, leaving some dinosaurs without food
Small animals eating dinosaurs eggs	Fewer dinosaurs reaching adulthood and reproducing
Major catastrophes or natural disruptions on Earth such as the rise of mountain chains, huge floods, or volcanic eruptions	Sudden death of plant and animal life
An asteroid or a comet striking Earth (Scientists believe that this actually may have happened.)	Dust thrown out from the impact – blocking out light and heat from the Sun for months or years, killing plants and causing large animals that ate plants or other animals to die, too
A nearby star exploding	Earth showered with deadly radiation such as X-rays

65   **Cretaceous Period**   **142**   **Jurassic Period**

Millions of Years Ago

Struthiomimus   *Pteranodon*   *Anatosaurus*   *Rhamphothorhynchus*

Allosaurus

Stegosaurus

Triceratops   *Tyrannosaurus*

Apatosaurus
(Brontosaurus)   *Archaeopteryx*

Ankylosaurus

A Pictorial Walk through Prehistory

Take a pictorial walk through prehistory. Our
walk begins at the left, 65 million years ago.
This is when dinosaurs disappeared from Earth.

Our walk ends at the far right, more than 400
million years ago, before there appeared on
Earth reptiles, the group of animals to which
dinosaurs belonged.

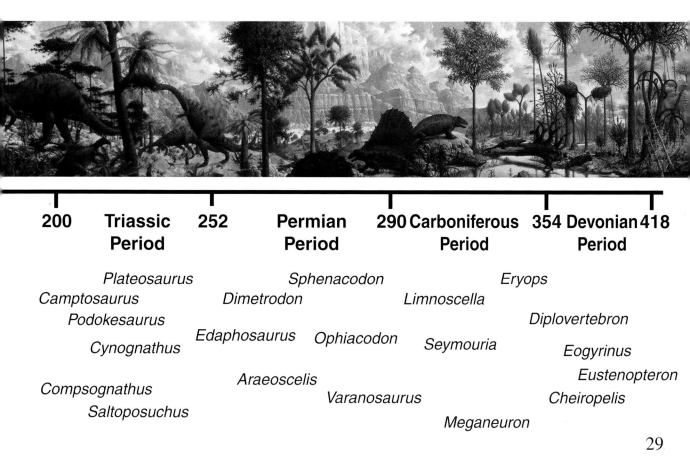

200	Triassic Period	252	Permian Period	290	Carboniferous Period	354	Devonian Period	418

Plateosaurus

Camptosaurus

Podokesaurus

Sphenacodon

Dimetrodon

Limnoscella

Eryops

Diplovertebron

Edaphosaurus *Ophiacodon*

Cynognathus

Seymouria

Eogyrinus

Eustenopteron

Araeoscelis

Compsognathus

Varanosaurus

Cheiropelis

Saltoposuchus

Meganeuron

29

More Books about Dinosaurs and Their Disappearance

Collision Course! Cosmic Impacts and Life on Earth. Fred Bortz (Millbrook Press)
Concise Dinosaur Encyclopedia. David Burnie (Larousse Kingfisher Chambers)
Dinosaurs A to Z: The Ultimate Dinosaur Encyclopedia. Don Lessem (Scholastic)
The End of the Dinosaurs. Rupert Matthews and Beatrice McLeod (Blackbirch)
Meteorite!: The Last Days of the Dinosaurs. Richard Norris (Raintree/Steck Vaughn)
National Geographic Dinosaurs. Paul Barrett (National Geographic)

Video

The Dinosaurs. (PBS Home Video)

Web Sites

The following sites on the Internet can help you learn about dinosaurs, about how they died out, and about objects from space that may strike Earth.

DinoData. www.dinodata.net/Discussions/dino/extinction.html

National Museum of Natural History (Smithsonian Institution): Blast from the Past. www.nmnh.si.edu/paleo/blast/

Planetary Society. www.planetary.org/html/neo/

Tunguska. www.galisteo.com/scripts/tngscript/default.prl

University of California Museum of Paleontology: DinoBuzz. www.ucmp.berkeley.edu/diapsids/dinobuzz.html

Views of the Solar System. www.solarviews.com/eng/tercrate.htm

Places to Visit

Here are some museums and centers where you can find a variety of exhibits about dinosaurs.

American Museum of Natural History
Central Park West at 79th Street
New York, NY 10024

Field Museum
1400 S. Lake Shore Drive
Chicago, IL 60605

Melbourne Museum
11 Nicholson St
Carlton, Victoria
Australia

Museum of Science
Science Park
Boston, MA 02114

National Museum of Natural History
Smithsonian Institution
10th Street and Constitution Ave. NW
Washington, DC 20560

Royal Ontario Museum
100 Queen's Park
Toronto, Ontario M5S 2C6
Canada

Glossary

asteroids: very small "planets." More than a milion of them exist in our Solar System. Most of them orbit the Sun between Mars and Jupiter, but there are thousands that travel near Earth.

billion: the number represented by 1 followed by nine zeroes — 1,000,000,000.

cold-blooded: having blood that changes temperature according to the temperature of the surroundings.

colony: a group of people settled in a place away from their original home.

comet: a small object in space made of ice, rock, and dust. When its orbit brings it closer to the Sun, it develops a tail of gas and dust.

crater: a hole or pit in the surface of a planet, such as Earth. It may be caused by the impact of an object or by a volcanic explosion.

evolve: to develop or change over a long period of time.

galaxy: a large star system containing up to hundreds of billions of stars, along with gas and dust. Our own galaxy is called the Milky Way.

geophysicist: a scientist who studies the features of Earth.

gravity: the force that causes objects like Earth and our Moon to be attracted to one another.

Halley's Comet: a comet named for English astronomer Edmond Halley that passes by Earth once every 76 years or so. Its most recent pass occurred in 1986.

iridium: a rare element that occurs more often in extraterrestrial objects such as asteroids than in Earth's crust.

meteor: a meteoroid that has entered Earth's atmosphere. Also, the bright streak of light made as the meteoroid enters or moves through the atmosphere. If the meteoroid lands on Earth, it is called a meteorite.

meteoroid: a lump of rock or metal drifting through space. Meteoroids can be as big as small asteroids or as small as specks of dust.

orbit: the path that one celestial object follows as it circles, or revolves around, another.

prehistory: the period in history before writing was used.

quarry: a large hole dug in the ground in order to extract a material such as stone.

Solar System: the Sun with the planets and all the other bodies, such as asteroids, that orbit the Sun.

Tyrannosaurus: a terrifying, meat-eating dinosaur.

vaporize: to turn something that is liquid or solid into a gas.

warm-blooded: having blood that stays about the same temperature regardless of the changing temperature.

Index

Born in 1920, Isaac Asimov came to the United States as a young boy from his native Russia. As a young man, he was a student of biochemistry. In time, he became one of the most productive writers the world has ever known. His books cover a spectrum of topics, including science, history, language theory, fantasy, and science fiction. His brilliant imagination gained him the respect and admiration of adults and children alike. Sadly, Isaac Asimov died shortly after the publication of the first edition of *Isaac Asimov's Library of the Universe.*

The publishers wish to thank the following for permission to reproduce copyright material: front cover, 3, 10-11, 13 (all), © Julian Baum; 4-5, 28-29, Rudolf Zallinger, Peabody Museum of Natural History; 6, 7, Terry Huseby, © *Discover Magazine*, March 1986; 8, © Allan E. Morton; 9 (both), Georg Gerster, Science Source; 12, 15, 24, © Mark Paternostro; 14, Leonid Kulik, courtesy of Smithsonian Institution; 16, © Michael Carroll 1994; 17, José R. Díaz, *Sky & Telescope* Magazine, © 1993 Sky Publishing Corp.; 18 (both), 19, 22 (both), 23, NASA/JPL; 20, © V. L. Sharpton/Lunar and Planetary Institute; 21 (upper), © Ron Miller; 21 (lower), 26, 27 (both), NASA; 25 (upper), Courtesy of European Southern Observatory; 25 (lower), © Michael Carroll.